Anger

by Laurie Beckelman

Series Consultant
John Livingstone, M.D.

Crestwood House
New York

Maxwell Macmillan Canada
Toronto

Maxwell Macmillan International
New York   Oxford   Singapore   Sydney

J'152.47
(1)

For Rob,
with thanks for remembering the
scratch marks with more love than anger

Author's Note:
Many teenagers generously shared their thoughts and experiences with me.
The quotes in this book are based on their stories.

Copyright © 1994 Crestwood House, Macmillan Publishing Company

Crestwood House
Macmillan Publishing Company
866 Third Avenue, New York, NY 10022

Maxwell Macmillan Canada, Inc.
1200 Eglinton Avenue East, Suite 200
Don Mills, Ontario M3C 3N1

Macmillan Publishing Company is part
of the Maxwell Communication Group of Companies.

First Edition
Design: Lynda Fishbourne, Hemenway Design Associates
Packaging: Prentice Associates Inc.
Photos:
Image Bank: Cover, 29, 35, PhotoEdit: (Mary Kate Denny) 4, 19, (Alan Oddie) 7,
(Richard Hutchings) 11, 31, (Tony Freeman) 14, 21, 39, (Freeman Grishaber) 24,
(David Young-Wolff) 16, 41, (Myrleen Ferguson Cate) 27, 44.

Printed in the United States of America
10 9 8 7 6 5 4 3 2 1

Library of Congress Cataloging-in-Publication Data
Beckelman, Laurie.
    Anger / by Laurie Beckelman.—1st ed.
        p. cm. — (Hot line)
    Includes bibliographical references and index.
    ISBN 0-89686-841-9   0-382-24744-2
    1. Anger—Juvenile literature. [1. Anger.] I. Title.
II. Series.
BF575.A5B43 1994
152.4'7—dc20   93-40641

Summary: A discussion of anger and how it affects relationships and self-esteem.
Provides examples of typical ways in which teens manage anger and offers suggestions
for managing anger more effectively.

HOT LINE

Anger

CONTENTS

No matter how we experience anger, it's what we do when we're angry that matters. Our response to anger affects our relationships and how we feel about ourselves.

The Electric Emotion

Do you get angry often?

No matter what you answered, you're not alone.

Perhaps you are like Marti, who says, "Well, sometimes I get mad, but I hate the feeling so I try not to show it."

Or maybe you are more like Derrick, who says he's angry "all the time, man, all the time."

Or perhaps Carmen's experience echoes your own: "We yell and scream a lot in my house—especially me and my sister. But it doesn't mean anything. Five minutes later we're best friends again."

Anger is as much a part of the normal human experience as eating or breathing. Everyone feels this emotion. But not everyone experiences it in the same way. For some people anger is as sharp as hunger pains. For others anger is as subtle as breathing—they get angry but hardly think about it.

Angry feelings make some people want to strike out. They make other people want to hide. But no matter how we experience anger, it's what we do when we're angry that matters. Our response to anger affects our relationships and how we feel about ourselves.

Anger is emotional electricity. Channeled well, it can light the bulb of understanding, helping us to see ourselves and our relationships more clearly. But left unchanneled, it can ruin friendships and strain family ties. It can make us feel out of control or unhappy with ourselves. At worst, it can explode into violence.

Many normal people have great trouble expressing anger in helpful ways. They have never learned to manage their anger. They may never have even learned that they *can* manage their anger. But they can, and so can you. You can learn to use anger to strengthen relationships rather than strain them. You can learn to change **anger habits** that keep you from feeling good about yourself. Changing anger habits, like changing any habit, is hard. But managing anger has many advantages.

In her book *Deadly Consequences*, the violence-prevention expert Deborah Prothrow-Stith makes a few important points:

■ People who take time to explore their differences usually learn to get along.

■ People who learn to resolve conflict nonviolently can generally avoid being bullies or victims. Kids who have the skills to stick up for themselves without using violence are strong. They don't need to bully others. And they can use their skills to quiet rather than inflame arguments.

■ Everyone in an argument can be a winner. When people talk problems through, they can come up with solutions that meet everyone's needs.

■ People who learn to settle arguments so that everyone wins feel better about themselves. When we can communicate, compromise, and settle our differences, we feel in control. This makes us feel good about ourselves.

These are gains well worth pursuing. This book shares many ideas for recognizing, understanding, and managing anger. By learning to manage anger, you can make its power your own.

People who learn to settle arguments so that everyone wins feel better about themselves.

Anger 101

All your life you have been in a class you never signed up for. Call it Anger 101. This class has taught you how to adapt to anger. When you were a toddler and threw a tantrum because you wanted ice cream, you were enrolled in Anger 101. If your mother gave in and got you the ice cream, you learned that throwing a tantrum gets you what you want. If she did not, you learned that tantrums don't work.

When you were a grade schooler and the teacher yelled at you for something you didn't do, you were attending Anger 101. If you tried to explain and she listened and apologized, you learned that sharing your point of view makes a difference. If she told you not to talk back and kept you in at recess, you learned that trying to explain is futile.

Each of us has had thousands of experiences like these. We've tested different responses to anger and seen what works. We've also learned by watching how those around us manage anger. Family members, friends, teachers, and siblings are among our models. If they bang pans, slam doors, and hurl insults at us when they are angry, we may grow up to lash out in anger, too. If they retreat into a black hole of brooding, we, too, may sulk and scowl when we're mad. We may punish others with our silence.

The media also teaches us. Movie and TV characters show us responses to anger each time they argue, fight, get even, or make peace. If Rambo is our hero, we may learn to prize violence. If we prefer Roseanne, humor may be our weapon of choice.

By the time we're teens, we've formed anger habits that are as second nature as brushing our teeth. Some of those habits serve us well. But others do not. Too often, we learn to use anger to get back at someone who has hurt, frustrated, or humiliated us. Or we learn to express our anger through fighting, running away, or smashing things. Such actions may or may not relieve our angry feelings, but they definitely do not solve the problems that made us angry. Some of us learn to ignore our anger or to avoid fights by blaming ourselves, not others, when we're mad at someone. This doesn't change what made us angry, either.

Often our anger habits follow our angry feelings so quickly that we confuse the two. "When I'm mad, it's pow! Fist lightning," says Derrick. "I mean, being angry *is* fighting. That's just the way it is." Like Derrick, many of us feel that the way we act when we are mad is "just the way it is." We think anger *is* yelling—or kicking, hitting, punching, or biting. But it isn't. It isn't crying, whining, blaming, pouting, dissing, or talking behind someone's back, either. And it isn't throwing books or destroying someone else's property or running away or even talking it through. All of these are behaviors. They are ways of responding to anger, but they are not anger itself. Anger itself is a feeling.

Separating angry feelings and angry actions is important because we can change angry actions. We can teach ourselves to become aware of our feelings and to choose how we act on them. Derrick says he often regrets striking out in anger. "Once I smashed my kid sister's favorite toy horse," he remembers. "Smashed it to pieces. And it wasn't even my sister I was mad at, man. I felt real bad. Real bad."

Luckily, habits that are learned can be unlearned. The first step in changing anger habits is to remember that they are not the same as angry feelings. The next step is to understand the value of angry feelings. Once you do, you will see why some ways of managing anger are more helpful than others.

Often our anger habits follow our angry feelings so quickly that we confuse the two. We think anger is yelling— or kicking, hitting, punching, or biting. But it isn't.

11

Why Get Angry?

"**I** wish I never got angry," says Marti. "It feels so bad, all I want to do is roll into a ball and hide."

Like Marti, many people hate the way they feel when they're mad. Rapid heart beats, tight throats, and tense muscles are uncomfortable. Crying, another common anger response, makes some people feel weak. Yet we all get angry. Indeed, research shows that most people feel angry once or twice a day. These uncomfortable feelings must serve some purpose!

They do. Anger is a warning that something is not right in our lives. It grabs us by the shoulder and says, *Hey! Pay attention! Something's wrong here.* For instance, Kira remembers flying into a rage at her friend Ellen over a little thing: Ellen wanted to borrow one of Kira's sweaters. "I really blew up, you know? I go, 'Forget it! I'm not your private shopping mall!' and Ellen goes, 'Well, ex-*cuse* me. I thought we were friends!' and storms off. Then I felt bad *and* mad," recalls Kira.

Kira couldn't understand her own anger. She'd lent Ellen clothing lots of times. Her anger made her wonder: Why do I feel this way?

As she thought about it, Kira realized she felt that Ellen always wanted something from her. Ellen had been her best friend during the summer, when she could swim in Kira's pool. But come September, Ellen hardly even called. Then Kira started going with Ron, and suddenly Ellen was her best friend again. It wasn't long before Ellen asked Kira to set her up with Ron's friend Paul. Kira realized that Ellen's request to borrow a sweater wasn't the real problem. It was only a symbol of what was wrong. Kira felt hurt and used. That's why she felt angry.

Anger prompted Kira to think about her relationship with Ellen more deeply. It helped her figure out what was wrong. Once she did, she could decide what to do. By thinking things through, Kira had used the power of anger to empower herself. She decided that she still wanted to be Ellen's friend, but she didn't want to be a friend of convenience.

But Kira had a problem. She'd thought all this through only *after* yelling at Ellen. Now Ellen was mad. She didn't want to speak to Kira.

When we express anger, we communicate our displeasure to others. Too often, we do so in ways that alienate us from each other. This is what happened to Kira and Ellen. But we can also express anger in ways that open dialogue and pave the way to greater understanding. When we do, we use the power of anger to strengthen our ties with those we love or care about.

When we express anger, we communicate our displeasure to others. Too often, we do so in ways that alienate us from each other.

Even when we have hurt someone with our anger, we can apologize and try again. That's what Kira did with Ellen. "I told her straight out, 'I felt really mad at you because I felt used,'" says Kira. "I told her what she'd done that made me feel this way, and she said, like, yeah, she could see how I felt. We had a good talk."

Of course, we don't always get angry at someone else. Sometimes we get angry at ourselves. Such anger can be a force for personal growth. It can help us see parts of ourselves we would like to change. But we don't always respond to ourselves in helpful ways, either.

Have you ever heard a voice like this in your head? "I can't believe you said that! You're so stupid. No wonder no one likes you." That's your **inner critic** talking. It's the voice inside that never thinks you're good enough, and it can rage at you in hurtful ways.

Like yelling or fighting, hurtful self-talk is an anger habit. And just as you can learn better ways to express anger at others, you can learn better ways to express anger at yourself. In order to do either, you need to drive a wedge between your angry feelings and your anger habits. That wedge is awareness. If you become aware of your angry feelings before they spill into anger habits, you can harness the power of anger. One useful way is to get to know your **anger triggers**, the types of comments and events that make you mad.

Parents or other care-takers are right up there on most teens' lists of top 10 anger triggers. But parents aren't the only ones.

Dissed, Hassled, and Hurt

"**M**y mother makes me *so* mad!" says Carmen. "I have this new boyfriend she doesn't like. So she keeps telling me what a jerk he is. She won't let me alone about him. The other day I got so mad I told her what I thought of *her* man, my stepfather. I mean, she didn't exactly choose Mr. Great Guy, so who's she to judge me?"

"My parents are very strict," says Adam. "They won't let me stay out as late as everyone else. They won't let me go to parties if adults aren't there. They won't let me hang out at the mall. They won't let me do anything!"

Parents or other caretakers are right up there on most teens' lists of top 10 anger triggers. But parents aren't the only ones. Kid brothers or sisters who get in our way or older ones who tease us, teachers who won't listen and friends who hurt us, teammates who can't win, strangers who are rude, adults who treat us as if we still were kids—they all can make us mad. So can jars we can't open and homework we can't do, or rules that seem senseless and situations that seem unjust.

The things that make us mad might seem to be very varied, but they actually have a lot in common. We can divide them into three main groups: rejections, frustrations, and injustices.

Rejections

When people reject us or disapprove of our choices, they assault our **self-esteem.** They open the door of self-doubt and let in the chill wind of insecurity. They make us wonder: Am I okay? Am I lovable? Can I make it on my own? These are questions most of us would rather not confront, so we slam the door shut with our anger. Our anger makes us feel powerful. It hides our insecurity.

In our teens we are first building a strong sense of who we are apart from our families. Our self-image is new and fragile. This insecurity about ourselves makes us very sensitive to rejection or disapproval. For instance, when Jorge didn't make his school's basketball team, he complained about the coach for days. The coach was prejudiced, Jorge said. He hadn't given Jorge a fair tryout. For Jorge, being angry with the coach was easier than facing his hurt feelings and the possibility that he wasn't good enough for the team.

When people reject us or disapprove of our choices, they assault our self-esteem. They open the door of self-doubt and let in the chill wind of insecurity. They make us wonder: Am I okay?

When parents or other caretakers reject or disapprove of us, we are especially quick to anger. This is because our relationships with them are so important. We need their approval. When her mom put down Carmen's boyfriend, the message she gave Carmen was: You can't make good choices for yourself. Carmen was outraged. Like most teens, she needed to make her own decisions. But she still needed her mother's approval. What was she to do?

Carmen may not have realized that her mother was confused and frustrated, too. She didn't know how to let Carmen make her own choices while still giving the guidance a parent should. She also felt rejected: Carmen didn't want her advice. Working out such conflicts is one of the toughest tasks teens and their families face.

Frustrations

We feel frustrated when we can't do something we think we should be able to do. "I build model planes," says Jeremy. "The other day I was working on one and I just couldn't get this part right. I got so mad that I threw it across the room." Because Jeremy prides himself on building model planes, his failure to fit that piece threatened his self-concept. He began to doubt his abilities, then he got mad. His anger hid his insecurity.

Mazie felt frustrated and furious when she couldn't do her bangs the way all the other girls in school did. She

felt like a failure at something that was easy for "everyone" else.

John felt a different kind of frustration. He ducked into the record store to buy a new CD on the way to soccer practice. But the checkout line was so long that he had to forget the CD. John cursed the cashier on the way out.

Things that frustrate our desires or make us doubt ourselves often make us mad. But they can challenge us, too. Jeremy didn't give up on his plane. He finished it. "I feel prouder of that plane than of any of the others because it was the hardest to do," he says. Mazie didn't give up, either. She realized that it wasn't her but her hair that was the problem. She found another hairstyle. And John made a promise to himself on the way to soccer practice. In the future, he'd try hard not to take his frustrations out on other people. He could tell the cashier that he was really frustrated with the long checkout line, but he shouldn't have attacked. After all, it wasn't the cashier's fault that the store was busy and John was pressed for time.

Injustices

Injustices are situations we feel are unfair. They come in more flavors than ice cream. When we do not get as much as we think we deserve—of anything from praise to opportunity to pizza—we feel unjustly treated. So, too, when we are wrongly accused or misunderstood. "My dad sat me down to talk about my report card," says Marti. "He goes, like, 'Marti, I can tell you're not working as hard as usual. Are there any problems you'd like to talk about?' I started to get real angry 'cause I *have* been working hard—the only 'problem' is that I have too much to do!"

Adam felt his parents were unfair, too. "They set such strict rules, it's like they don't trust me to take care of myself," he says. Adam, like many teens, feels ready for more responsibility than his parents will allow.

Laura relates a different experience with injustice.

"Becca, this really popular girl in my class? Well, she suddenly starts talking to me. She invited me over to her house and everything. But then, like, I saw her walking with her friend Karen and ran to catch up. I was just about to call out to her when I hear her go, 'You think I really *like* Laura? Give me a break. She's a dork. But she's really good in math. I figured I could get her to do my homework for me.'" Laura felt used, hurt, humiliated, and mad.

Like frustration, injustice can prompt us to turn anger into positive action. We can do this in our personal lives: Adam got up enough courage to talk to his parents about changing some of their rules; Laura took the one positive thing Becca had said (that Laura was good in math) and used it to her advantage. She joined her school's math club.

We can also use anger at injustice as a force for change in our schools and communities. Many people are angered by **social injustice**. They see situations in society they believe are wrong and should be changed. The civil rights movement, the women's movement, and the gay rights movement all grew out of anger at social injustices. "Where I live you see a lot of homeless people," says Charlene. "It makes me so mad. *No one* should have to live like that!" Charlene joined a group at her church that assists homeless people. She is using her rage at injustice to help bring about change.

Getting to know your anger triggers is an important step in learning how to manage anger. So is recognizing how your body feels when you are mad.

Know Your Anger Triggers

Different things trigger anger for different people. You might laugh off an insult that infuriates your friend. Your friend may fume when he's kept waiting, while you think it's no big deal.

Try this exercise to identify your own anger triggers. Write this sentence starter at the top of a piece of paper: "I get angry when . . ." Then complete it with the first eight things that come to mind. Write quickly, without censoring your thoughts. Write exactly what comes to mind, no matter how silly it may seem. **Psychologists** Nathaniel and E. Devers Branden suggest that you do this exercise each night for six nights. Then, on the seventh night, complete this sentence starter: "I am becoming more aware that . . ." This sentence-starter activity can help you get to know your anger triggers.

Getting to know your anger triggers is an important step in learning how to manage anger. So is recognizing how your body feels when you are mad.

Your Angry Body

Carmen: Anger starts in my stomach, this real nervous-like feeling.

Derrick: Everything gets tight, man. I want to explode.

Marti: My heart feels like it's doing jumping jacks!

As Carmen's, Derrick's, and Marti's descriptions suggest, anger isn't all in the mind. It is a feeling rooted in the body. Anger sounds an alarm. It puts the body on alert, preparing it to respond to a threat. That threat can be physical—a sister using her nails as knives, for example. But more often the threat is emotional. People or events that make us feel unsure of ourselves, that treat us unfairly, or that frustrate our efforts to move forward in the world can threaten our emotional safety.

Your body responds to these **psychological stresses** in much the same way it responds to physical danger. This response, called the **fight-or-flight response**, is as old as the human species. It originated when most of the threats humans met *were* physical. Its purpose is to provide the extra energy your body needs to face danger. Here's what happens.

When the brain senses a need for extra energy, it sends out chemical messengers, called **hormones**, to prepare the body to respond. Like runners from head-quarters bringing news to generals in the field, these hormones alert other body systems to prepare for action. They activate the **adrenal glands** and the **sympathetic nervous system** (SNS).

Anger sounds an alarm. It puts the body on alert, preparing it to respond to a threat.

The adrenals and SNS slow down those body functions that won't help meet the emergency and speed up those that will. Extra sugar, the body's fuel, flows from the **liver** into the blood, and breathing becomes deeper and more rapid. These changes provide fuel for extra energy and the oxygen needed to burn that fuel.

At the same time, heart rate and blood pressure increase, speeding the oxygen- and sugar-rich blood to where it is needed. The blood vessels leading to the brain and to the large muscles in the arms and legs widen, allowing more blood to move through. Blood vessels into the stomach narrow and digestion stops—you can face an emergency on a full stomach but not with weak muscles or a sluggish brain! Other changes occur, too. Your pupils dilate so that you can see better and you become more alert, watchful, and anxious. You are ready to fight or flee.

Unfortunately, fighting or fleeing is not the best response to most situations that make us angry today. Yet this is what our body prepares us to do. And it prepares us so well that the tension we feel can seem intolerable. If we haven't learned other ways to relieve the tension, it can push us into action. We may cry, run, hit, screech—anything that will stop our uncomfortable feelings.

This can be most true in adolescence. The internal changes that are giving your body its adult shape are also giving you greater amounts of aggressive energy. You might find yourself getting angry more easily and with greater force than you did when you were a kid. This frightens some teens. It makes others feel powerful. It challenges all teens to learn how to make these strong feelings work for rather than against them.

Fighting or fleeing is not the best response to most situations that make us angry. There are other ways, such as sports, to relieve our tension.

Know Your Angry Body

You know that a pounding heart, tight muscles, burning cheeks, and a nervous stomach can signal anger. So you can tune into your body at the first sign of these symptoms and do an anger check.

Ask yourself, is something here making me mad? Am I frustrated? Is something unfair? Do I feel rejected? If the answer is yes, acknowledge that you are angry. Then take a moment to chill out. How to do this? The best advice is old advice:

■ Count to 10—or to 100.

■ Take a deep breath. Breathe in deeply through your nose, then breathe out slowly through your mouth.

■ If you can walk away to calm down, do. Sometimes channeling anger into sports, creative projects, or other activities helps. Doing a useful activity gives you time to cool down and to think about what's really bugging you.

These time-honored techniques help calm your aroused nervous system. You can teach yourself other ways to chill out, too. Many books describe **relaxation techniques**. These are exercises that help you relax your muscles. They take practice, but people who become good at them are able to relax in tense situations. Such exercises might help you, too.

If something makes you angry when your body is already keyed up, you may react more strongly than usual. Your anger may be harder to control.

Another important thing to know is that anger is not the only emotion that prepares your body for action. Your body has a one-size-fits-all response to stressful situations. Any situation—even a good one—that might require extra energy triggers the same response. Emotions as different as joy, anxiety, and anger all prepare your body for action. Social pressures, loud noises, crowding, and exercise can, too.

If something makes you angry when your body is already keyed up, you may react more strongly than usual. Your anger may be harder to control. Drugs, alcohol, hunger, and fatigue also make anger harder to manage.

So when you feel as if you're going to blow, stop and think about what might be adding to your feelings. Is the music blaring? Have you just finished a 5-mile run? Are you nervous about a date? Are you revved up on coffee or cola? If so, lower the music. Take 5 minutes to cool down from your run. Recognize that date jitters or caffeine may be making you overreact.

Thinking before you act is not easy. It takes practice. But it is a skill you can learn, just like swimming or sewing or riding a bike. And it helps. When you understand why your body feels as it does, you are better able to turn angry feelings to good use. And when you know your anger habits, you can change those you don't like. You can learn new ways to act on those feelings.

Word Wars and Silent Suffering

"**W**hen my dad was getting on me about my report card, I started getting mad," says Marti. "But then I thought, he's probably right. I probably should be trying harder. But how?" Marti felt angry at herself: Why couldn't she work harder? But she also felt confused: She *was* working hard! She wasn't sure what was right.

Marti's response is an example of one of four main types of anger habits. Here's a description of each one.

Silent suffering. Sometimes we choose not to express anger. We may "swallow our anger," not letting anyone know how we feel. Or, like Marti, we may turn our anger inward, blaming ourselves instead of the person who made us mad.

Of course, our silence isn't always silent. Sometimes it yells, "I am angry!" as loudly as words. We may scowl, slam our books down, refuse to talk. When we give others the silent

33

treatment, we let them know that we're mad. But we close the door on resolving our differences.

Word wars. We may yell, scream, blame, or slash someone with a verbal knife when we are mad. We may dredge up every past hurt and point out every one of their failings to prove how bad our opponents are and how wronged we feel. "When my mom and I were fighting about my boyfriend and I told her what I thought of my stepfather, I really got to her," says Carmen. "She just glared at me, then left the room. I'm not sure, but I think maybe she was crying. I felt kind of good at first, like, wow—I really showed her! But I don't know . . . then I felt guilty."

Like Carmen, many of us feel good at first when we let off steam or "win" an angry war of words. We feel powerful, in control. But the feeling rarely lasts. Winning battles this way doesn't win the war—it doesn't solve the problems that made us mad.

Violence. Smashing things, punching holes in walls, hitting or otherwise attacking someone else are all violent responses to anger. "This guy starts dissin' me at lunch, right? So I give it right back to him," says Derrick. "Next thing, he's pushin' me and I'm pushin' right back. Man, if the bell didn't ring, one of us would've got knifed."

Sometimes we choose not to express anger. We may "swallow our anger," not letting anyone know how we feel. Or we may turn our anger inward, blaming ourselves.

Today, too many kids aren't saved by the bell. Homicide is the second leading cause of death among teens. Anger isn't always the cause of violence, but it is often enough. Too many teens have not learned nonviolent ways to show angry feelings. They don't know of any other options, so they turn to violence—even though they know its dark side.

In a violence-prevention course she gives, Deborah Prothrow-Stith has kids list what's good and what's bad about fighting. You can try this, too. Like the students in Dr. Prothrow-Stith's classes, you'll probably think of more that's bad than good. Like yelling and screaming, violence can relieve angry feelings. It can make us feel powerful for a while, but that feeling rarely lasts. In the long run, violence does not make us feel as good inside as does being masters of our emotions.

Talking. Talking things through is often the best way to resolve anger. But how and when we talk makes a difference. Some people find that they can't talk when they're really mad. They need to cool down first (see pages 30-31 for some strategies for chilling out). Others find waiting intolerable. They need to solve the problem *now*. Neither way is right or wrong. What matters is what works for you.

How we talk matters, too. If the goal of expressing anger is to communicate, we need to find ways of letting off steam without burning other people. Talk that attacks ("You're so selfish!"), that blames and accuses ("Now look what you've done! You've ruined my best shirt!"), is a word war. Talk that simply rehashes the problem in the same way, over and over, doesn't work, either. It's like riding a stationary bicycle. You don't get anywhere.

Talk that goes one way, so only one person's point of view is heard, doesn't communicate well, either. Often both people in an argument feel wronged. They can't resolve their hurt feelings unless both are heard. If they are heard, they may feel better even if they haven't solved anything. Learning how to talk so people will listen and listen so people will talk is an important skill. It is the key to communication. And communication is the key to changing many of the situations that make us angry. (See pages 42-44 for some tips on how to express your feelings without attacking).

Know Your Anger Habits

Think about the last time you were angry with a friend, a parent, a teacher. What did you do? What did you say? Chances are, you respond differently to anger at different times and with different people. Maybe you fume silently when you're angry with your parents but scream at your sister. Perhaps you give one friend the cold shoulder but talk things through with another. Maybe you bite your tongue when a teacher yells at you, but you pick a fight with the first kid who looks at you wrong.

Research shows that most people have different anger habits in different situations. For example, few adults yell at their bosses, but many yell at their children or spouses. They may *feel* angry with their bosses, but they choose not to express their feelings because doing so could get them fired.

One good way to get to know your anger habits is to keep an anger diary for a while. Get a notebook, then divide each sheet of paper into columns with the following heads: Who, Where, Why, What, The Deeper Feeling.

At the end of each day, make some anger notes. Write down who you got angry with, where it happened, why you got mad, what you did, what the effect was, and what you think the deeper feeling was (were you feeling hurt? used? frustrated? fearful?). You'll start to see patterns to your anger. This will help you decide which anger habits work for you and which you might want to change.

At the end of each day, make some anger notes. You'll start to see patterns to your anger.

What Works

"**I** got really mad when this girl made fun of my hair," says Mazie. "But then I thought, so what? She's not my friend, anyway. Besides, she looks like she used three cans of hairspray this morning. Who wants to look like that?"

"This guy? The one I got in the fight with at lunch? Well, he starts in on me again after school," says Derrick. "And I don't know, I just wasn't in the mood. So I try walkin' away, but he comes after me. Calls me a yellow-bellied chicken—. So I go, 'Oh, my! I must've forgot to turn over at the tanning sa-lon.' Cracked everyone right up. So then his friend goes, 'Come on, man, leave him be.' And that ended it." Derrick says he felt surprisingly good after this happened. He hadn't known that not fighting could make him feel strong.

"My friend's dad offered to take a bunch of us to a pro hockey game in town," says Alex. "I was so psyched. But when I told my mom, she said, 'Hockey? No way.' I stormed out of the house. Rode my bike as fast as I could. But when I calmed down, I decided I couldn't let her do this to me. I went home and told my mom we needed to talk."

Mazie, Derrick, and Alex responded to anger in three different ways. Each response was right for the situation. Silence or humor that doesn't attack is often the best response to bullies and teases. Anger that reflects our own fatigue or mood more than what the other person did is usually best left unexpressed.

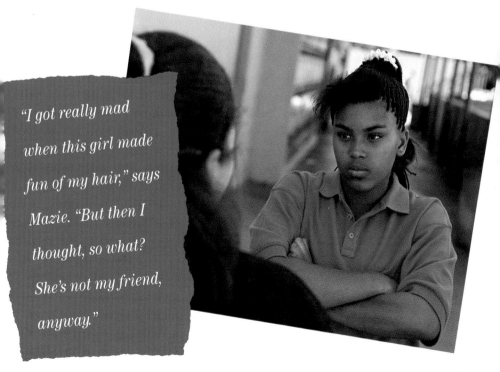

"I got really mad when this girl made fun of my hair," says Mazie. "But then I thought, so what? She's not my friend, anyway."

But anger aroused by major problems or misunder-
standings, such as Alex's conflict with his mom, is rarely
resolved through silence. It doesn't just go away. It can
make us feel bad about ourselves. And sometimes it can
come out in self-destructive ways—overeating, drug use,
delinquency. This type of anger is best handled through
talking.

Talking so people will listen means expressing your
feelings without attacking. **Psychiatrist** John B.
Livingstone suggests several techniques:

■ Use **"I" statements**. "I feel used and get really mad
when you take my stuff without asking" doesn't attack.
"You're such a pig" does. Which would you rather hear?

■ Search for the hurt or fear behind the anger. Use your
angry feelings as a signal that something deeper may be
wrong. Ask yourself, "What's really hurting or threatening
me?" If you can, express the deeper feelings.

■ Try **active listening**. When you use this technique, you
listen without interrupting and repeat to yourself what
the other person is saying. The old cliché "Every argument has two sides" is true. Rarely is one person totally
"wrong" and the other person totally "right." More often,
the two people have conflicting needs or viewpoints. For
example, Alex's parents feel the need to protect him,

while he feels the need for more freedom and responsibility. If they don't listen—really listen—to each other's needs, they won't be able to find a compromise. Also, if Alex understands his parents' real concerns, he may feel less angry. He'll have more energy to put into solving his problem. Often, feeling listened to is enough to calm people down, even if they still disagree.

■ Let people know you're listening accurately by repeating what they've said. If Alex says, "So you're saying you're afraid I'll get hurt if I go to the hockey game," he lets his mother know that he understands her concerns even if he disagrees with them. If he's got it wrong, she can try to explain again. Ask that the person you're speaking with do the same.

■ Let people know you care or respect them even though you're mad. This helps them accept your anger. And when our feelings are accepted, we usually feel better. Talking to yourself with love and respect is a good idea, too. Remember, hurtful self-talk is as much an anger habit as hurtful talk directed at others. When you yell at yourself, you undermine the confidence you need to take control and change the things that make you mad.

■ If you get "stuck" in an argument, say so: "I think we're stuck." Then try to cool it for a while or to see the problem in a new way. We often feed our anger by playing the same thoughts over and over, as if they were a favorite record. By moving on to a new song, we may be able to cut through conflict to resolution. Ask yourself, "What do I want?" "What am I trying to fix with my anger?" If you figure it out, tell the other person.

■ Apologize. If you have hurt someone with your anger, say you're sorry. Apologizing isn't the same as saying that the other person was right and you were wrong. It's simply a way to acknowledge that the other person is hurt or upset. We all need to have our feelings acknowledged. As you've already learned, when we feel heard and understood, we often feel less angry. Perhaps if you apologize to others, they will find it easier to do the same for you.

When we feel heard and understood, we often feel less angry, even if nothing has changed.

A Final Word

The Institute for Mental Health Initiatives has developed an easy way to remember many of the strategies described in this book. When you start to get angry, **RETHINK:**

Recognize that you are angry. Try to label and express your angry feelings.

Empathize with the other person. Try to see the situation from his or her point of view. What is he or she feeling? thinking? Have you ever had similar feelings?

Think about the situation in a new way. How we think about a problem influences how we feel about it and the options we see for solving it. By trying to see the humor or challenge in a situation, for example, we can often move beyond anger to problem solving. Try, too, to think about how you may be contributing to the problem.

Hear what the other person is saying. Check to make sure you understand correctly by mirroring back what the person has said. Let someone talk without interrupting. If the other person seems to be finished, check by asking, "Is there more?"

Integrate respect or love with what you say. Direct expressions of respect or caring, active listening, and "I" statements that communicate your feelings without blaming are ways of doing this.

Notice what works to help you control your anger. Taking a deep breath, going for a long walk, catching a movie, asking for a hug, shooting hoops, and many other things can relieve angry feelings. Find out what works for you and use it.

Keep your attention on the present. Bringing up old grudges and past hurts usually increases anger.

By RETHINKing anger, you can control your anger instead of letting it control you. By RETHINKing anger, you can claim anger's power as your own. Good luck!

If You'd Like to Learn More

Organizations
The following groups provide information on anger or violence.

Institute for Mental Health Initiatives
Channeling Children's Anger
4545 42nd Street, NW, Suite 311
Washington, DC 20016
202-364-7111

National Association for Mediation in Education
425 Amity Street
Amherst, MA 01002
413-545-2462

Books and Movies
Books and movies can help us understand our feelings better.
Here are some that deal with anger.

Face to Face by Marion Dane Bauer (New York: Clarion Books,
1991). Picked on at school by bullies, 13-year-old Michael
confronts his fears and anger during a trip to visit the father
he has not seen in eight years.

When You're Mad, Mad, Mad! Dealing with Anger
(Pleasantville, NY: Sunburst, 1993). This short video demon-
strates positive strategies for expressing anger toward parents,
friends, and events.

Work It Out, Talk It Out (Washington, DC: Institute for Mental
Health Initiatives, 1988). This video uses music, role playing,
and discussion to demonstrate the RETHINK approach to
managing anger.

Glossary/Index